1000

Conversation Questions

Designed for use in the ESL or EFL Classroom

Discussion questions were used with the permission of ESL Conversation Questions
www.eslconversationquestions.com

Published by ECQ Publishing

Printed in the United States of America

First Printing, 2012

ISBN-10: 1942116055
ISBN-13: 978-1942116059

Distributed by
CreateSpace
4900 LaCross Road
North Charleston, SC 29406
USA
www.createspace.com/pub/l/createspacedirect.do

Second Edition

ACKNOWLEDGMENTS 9

EXTRAS 10

    Bonus questions and topics 10

    Our other books 10

    Join our reviewer program 10

USING CONVERSATION QUESTIONS IN THE CLASSROOM 11

    Timing 11

    Group size 11

    Mistakes are okay 12

    Let the conversation flow 12

    Keep out of the discussion 13

    Take notes 13

CONVERSATION QUESTIONS 14

    Adoption 15

    Advice 16

    Aging 17

    Aliens 18

    Animals 19

    Appearance 20

    Architecture/Building Design 21

    Art 22

    Beauty 23

    Books 24

    Brains 25

    Camping 26

    Cars and Driving 27

Challenges..28

Change...29

Charity...30

Choices..31

Cities...32

Cleanliness...33

Cloning..34

Collectibles..35

Color...36

Communication..37

Computers...38

Conspiracies and Cover Ups..39

Cooking...40

Corruption...41

Creativity...42

Crime..43

Customs...44

Dating...45

Disabilities...46

Dreaming...47

Drugs..48

Eating Habits...49

Electric Cars..50

Email...51

Empathy..52

Entrepreneurs..53

Environmental Problems 54

Ethics 55

Facts and Statistics 56

Family 57

Family Values 58

Fashion 59

Fast Food 60

First Impressions 61

The Five Senses 62

Food 63

Free Time 64

Friendship 65

Fruits and Vegetables 66

Future 67

Games 68

Getting a Job 69

Glasses and Contacts 70

Golf 71

Habits 72

Having Children 73

Health 74

History 75

Hobbies 76

Holidays 77

Homes 78

Hotels 79

Human Wonders 80

Humor 81

Idols 82

Immigration 83

Individuality 84

Intelligence 85

The Internet 86

Investing 87

Jobs 88

Languages 89

Learning English 90

Love 91

Luck 92

Luxury Items 93

Manners 94

Marriage 95

Massage 96

The Media 97

Medicine 98

Meeting New People 99

Memory 100

Money 101

Motivation 102

Movies 103

Multiple Intelligences 104

Music 105

Natural Disasters...106

Natural Wonders..107

Neighborhoods...108

Neighbors..109

News...110

Numbers...111

Online Dating..112

The Past..113

Past Ability...114

Personality..115

Pets..116

Photography...117

Police...118

Privacy...119

Productivity..120

Remedies...121

Responsibility...122

Restaurants...123

Retirement..124

Science...125

Seasons..126

Secrets...127

Shopping...128

Singing..129

Single Life...130

Sleep..131

Smoking 132

Sports 133

Stories 134

Stress 135

Success and Failure 136

Super Heroes 137

The Supernatural 138

Technology 139

Television 140

Tipping 141

Tourism 142

Transitions 143

Travel 144

University 145

Water 146

Weddings 147

Wishes 148

ENJOY THE BOOK? 149

Check out our other books 149

Or why not leave a review? 149

We love feedback! 149

ACKNOWLEDGMENTS

There are a few people I would like to thank for their help in getting me to the point where I could write this book.

First of all, I would like to thank my parents, Larry and Lona, and my brother Wesley. Without their love, infinite patience, guidance, and understanding I would have never made it as far as I have.

I want to thank my wife for her encouragement and love throughout all my successes and failures.

I would also like to thank all of my fellow teachers who have kept me sane through the hard times and celebrated with me during the good times.

Lastly, I want to thank all of my students who have made my years of teaching fun and interesting.

EXTRAS

There are just a couple of extras I want to let you know about before you start using this book.

Bonus questions and topics

The title would have you believe that there are 1000 questions in this book, but the truth is there are actually more than that.

There is actually a grand total of 1436 questions spanning 134 topics in this book. Enjoy the extra topics and questions!

Our other books

If you are not already aware, we also publish several other books for ESL teachers. Here are some of the other books we have created:

ESL Role Plays: 50 Engaging Role Plays for ESL and EFL Classes

500 Grammar Based Conversation Questions

ESL Worksheets and Activities for Kids

IELTS Study Guide: Tips, Tricks, and Strategies

Join our reviewer program

We are always looking for qualified reviewers for our books. But we don't want to offer free review copies to just anyone. We want to offer them to people who are more likely to leave a review since they have left reviews in the past.

So if you leave a review of this book and are interested in receiving a free digital copy of one of our books as a review copy, let me know which of the reviews is yours and which book you are interested in at:

larrypitts@eslconversationquestions.com

We only ask that you actually review the review copy we send you. Once you write a review of the book we sent you, we can send you a digital review copy of another one of our books.

We'll also send you a review copy of any new books we come out with.

USING CONVERSATION QUESTIONS IN THE CLASSROOM

Let me begin by saying, these tips on how to use conversation questions in the classroom are based on what I have found to work in my classes. You may have to tweak or disregard some of my advice to accommodate your own teaching style. With that in mind, let's get started.

Timing

First, let's talk about how much time to allocate for questions. When planning lessons, I most often follow a rough rule of a minimum of one minute per question and a maximum of three minutes per question. That doesn't really indicate how much time they will spend on each individual question; it's just a rough estimate for judging the amount of time it will take to finish a set of questions.

So, if you give your students ten questions, you'll burn between ten to thirty minutes of class time. Now of course this isn't a steadfast rule. There will always be exceptions. All things considered though, about twenty minutes for ten questions is the average for my classes.

Another quick point, if you can limit how many questions they see at a time (using PowerPoint or spaced handouts) they will answer questions more fully and take more time. I find showing them five questions at a time makes for a good pace.

Group size

Next, you need to decide how many students to put into each group. As a general rule of thumb I find that three students in a group is the ideal number. I say this because with three students everyone gets a good chance to talk, but there are still enough people to have a rich reservoir of ideas to discuss.

Two students really maximize talking time, but often the two students don't get along or you might have two shy students that end up together.

Four students can work, but often there isn't enough talk time for each student and shy students feel like they are on stage every time they talk.

Five students in a group are far too many and often they just won't talk. All this being said, ultimately it comes down to the dynamics of your class and its size.

If you have a really talkative class with a good dynamic, putting them in pairs works well. Groups of four generally work best with groups of shy students, because they feel more pressure to speak if everyone in the group is silent.

Mistakes are okay

Assure your students that mistakes are okay. If they aren't making mistakes, they aren't trying hard enough. Tell them that you are happy when they make mistakes because that means they are trying new and difficult ways of saying things. If they don't make any mistakes then they haven't learned anything.

One thing to stress is that they shouldn't be speaking their native language. It is better to say something that is incorrect or unclear in English than correctly and clearly in their first language.

Let the conversation flow

Another important point to stress is that they are free to discuss more than just the questions. In a natural conversation the topic moves from one subject to another; this is what you want in your classes as well. Very often students will treat questions like an ordered set of goals to accomplish. Let them know if they don't discuss them all, that's okay!

If they spend the whole time talking about just one question, that is great. It means they are having a natural conversation. Just make sure they are speaking only in English! I tell my students that they can discuss whatever questions they think are interesting. If they don't think any questions are interesting, they should make their own questions.

I let them know that I don't care what they talk about, as long as they speak in English. Now that isn't totally true, I do care about what they talk about, and I target my questions to accomplish certain goals in the class. But I want them to feel free enough to branch off into a natural conversation. I would say 99% of the time they just use the questions that I give them. How about the other 1%? Well at least they are speaking English, and they usually get to the questions eventually.

Keep out of the discussion

After you have put the students into groups and they are talking, there is one important point to remember. Stay out of the discussion! I know it may be tempting to make a comment, but this is their time to discuss.

The only time you should be interrupting their discussion is when they ask you for help. Sometimes you can interject with a vocabulary word if they are searching for the perfect word or if they are using a vocabulary word incorrectly over and over again. Otherwise, stay out of the discussion. So what are you doing while they are discussing? You are monitoring each group's discussion and taking notes.

Take notes

While you are monitoring your students' discussions, you should be taking notes. Take note of any errors that are being made repeatedly (i.e., errors in grammar, pronunciation, or vocabulary use). Write down some specific sentences that contain common errors you hear or that contain errors you wish to work on.

Decide which errors or mistakes would be useful to go over with the class and at the end of class or at the end of the discussion, go over some of these mistakes and errors. When you go over the errors, keep them anonymous and let students know that it's a good thing if they see their mistake on the board. You might let the class try to correct the errors or correct them yourself for the class depending on how much time you have.

So, those are the tips I have for using conversation questions in an adult ESL class. You may find that these tips don't suit your teaching style. Give them a try and if they don't mesh with your teaching style, try something different. Every teacher teaches differently and every student learns differently. Ultimately the goal is to find what works best for you and your class.

CONVERSATION QUESTIONS

Adoption

- How is adoption viewed in your country?

- Do you know anyone who was adopted? Can you think of any famous people who were adopted?

- How does being adopted affect a child's view of themselves?

- What are some of the reasons people adopt children?

- What are some of the reasons people give children up for adoption?

- What do you think about the adoption system in your country?

- What do you think about couples that adopt children from different countries?

- What qualities make a couple or a person qualified to adopt a child?

- Should the adoption process be more, or less, difficult than it is now?

- Should people be able to decide what type of children they want to adopt? For example: boy or girl, hair color, age, etc.

Advice

- What three pieces of advice will you give your children?

- Whose advice do you follow more, your parents' or your friends' advice?

- If you could give the leader of your country some advice, what would it be?

- If you could go back in time and give yourself some advice, what would you tell your younger self?

- Who was the wisest person in your country's history? What kind of advice did they give?

- Where do you go to get good advice?

- How often do you give your friends advice? What advice do you give them?

- Tell your partner a problem you have and let them give you advice.

- What advice can you give to someone who wants to make the world a better place?

- If a business man, a scientist, and a religious scholar gave you different advice about a problem, whose advice would you follow?

Aging

- What are some of the benefits of getting older?

- Do you think humans will ever be able to stop aging?

- Is aging more difficult for men or women? Why?

- Which celebrities have aged well?

- Are older people actually wiser?

- What kind of support should children give their aging parents?

- How long do you want to live?

- Who is the oldest person you know? How is their view of the world different than yours?

- How are older people viewed in your country?

- How well do you relate to people who are five years younger than you? How about ten years younger?

Aliens

- Do you believe there is any other life in the universe? How about intelligent life?

- What do you think aliens might look like?

- Do you think aliens have ever visited earth?

- Have you seen a UFO or do you know someone who has seen a UFO?

- What is your favorite alien from a movie?

- What is the scariest alien movie?

- If aliens did come to a country and met with the government of that country, what do you think would happen?

- Why are humans so fascinated by aliens?

- How many planets do you think are in our galaxy? How about the universe?

- Do you think humans will travel to another planet in your lifetime?

- How do you think we or aliens will get to other star systems like our own?

Animals

- What animal best represents you? Why?

- What creature scares you? Why?

- Except for food, do humans need other animals? Why or why not?

- What is the most effective way to save endangered species?

- What are some examples of useful traits that help animals survive? (i.e., a giraffe's long neck)

- What is Darwin famous for?

- What traits have made humans a successful species?

- What is the cutest animal you can think of? How about the ugliest?

- Why do humans have pets? Do you have a pet? Why or why not?

- Are there any animals that we should try to kill off completely?

Appearance

- What is the first thing you notice about a person?

- What do the clothes someone wears say about that person?

- Is there a part of your appearance that you are very proud of? (Eyes, fashion sense, hair, etc.)

- What is the most interesting haircut you have seen?

- Have you ever gone through the entire day without noticing something was wrong with your appearance? (i.e., missing button, food in your teeth)

- What kinds of things do you do to improve/maintain your appearance?

- Are there any fashion trends in the past you followed but are embarrassed about now?

- How long does it take you to get ready in the morning?

- Have you ever been intimidated by someone's appearance?

- Do people in your country talk a lot about other people's appearance?

- Is it rude to tell a person that they need to improve their appearance?

Architecture/Building Design

- What kinds of materials are buildings made from?

- Is there one type of building material you prefer in buildings?

- What kind of style of buildings do you like? (Traditional, modern, crazy, functional, etc.)

- What do you think of your country's modern/traditional architecture?

- What are some buildings around where you live that you like?

- Is it better to build concrete block buildings that are cheap, easy to build, and all look the same or more expensive buildings that have varied designs?

- Talk about the construction industry and real estate industry in your country.

- There are many types of houses (underground, eco-friendly, rural, apartment). What kind of house would be your ideal house?

- How much does architecture affect people's moods?

- Have you ever been interested in architecture?

- What makes a good interior for a restaurant? Office? Home? Classroom?

- Smart buildings are being built now that can do lots of things. What would you like to see buildings be able to do in the future?

Art

- How often do you go to art museums?

- Do you consider yourself to be artistic?

- What do you think about modern art paintings?

- How many forms of art can you name? What is your favorite form of art?

- Is graffiti art? Why or why not?

- What is the most famous statue in your country?

- Who is your favorite artist? Why do you like them so much?

- Do you think that art is important to society? Why?

- Have you ever tried drawing, painting, sculpting, or something else artistic?

- What is the most famous painting in your country?

- What is traditional art like in your culture?

- What country do you think is the most creative?

- Why is art so expensive? Do you think it should be more or less expensive?

- Do you have any artistic friends? What kinds of art do they create?

Beauty

- Do you think beauty is the same for every person?

- Do you think that different cultures think about beauty differently?

- What do you think of plastic surgery?

- What is the most common plastic surgery in your country?

- What does "Beauty is only skin deep" mean?

- What kinds of beauty contests are popular in your country? Do they have beauty contests for men, too?

- What celebrities do you know of that have gotten plastic surgery?

- Who is the most beautiful/handsome celebrity in your country?

- What makes someone beautiful?

- Do you think science can measure beauty?

Books

- Do you read many books?

- How often do you read books?

- Did your parents read to you when you were a child?

- What are some of the advantages of books versus movies? How about the disadvantages of books versus movies?

- What was the last book you read and what was it about?

- Do you prefer fiction or non-fiction books?

- Do you think people don't read enough books these days?

- If you could only read one book for the rest of your life, what would it be?

- Can a book change the world?

- Who is an author that you like? Why do you like their books?

- What are some examples of traditional literature in your country? Did you have to read it in school?

- Do you like reading the traditional literature of your country?

Brains

- What is the most amazing thing about the brain?

- What are some extraordinary things some people can do with their brains?

- Will we ever be able to augment our brain with technology? Would you augment your brain?

- What do you wish your brain was better at?

- Do you think male and female brains are better at different tasks? Why or why not?

- What is the most mysterious aspect of the brain?

- What do you think about most?

- What does your brain do that you hate?

- Do you think humans will ever completely understand the brain? Why or why not?

- When do you use your brain the most?

Camping

- What is the best activity to do while camping?

- How many times have you gone camping? Did you enjoy it?

- Where have you gone camping?

- What are the four most important things to bring when you go camping?

- Is camping with lots of amenities (solar panels, fans, stove, etc.) still camping? How much luxury is too much?

- Where is the best place to go camping in your country?

- What is the longest time you have spent camping?

- Tell a story about a camping trip (it doesn't have to be your story).

- What is the best thing about camping? How about the worst thing?

- What is the best food to bring on a camping trip?

Cars and Driving

- If you were going to get a new car, what kind of car would you get? A luxury car? A sports car? A hybrid or electric car?

- What kinds of cars do you think look the best?

- Can you drive? If you can drive, are you a good driver? When did you get your license? If you can't drive, do you want to get a driver's license? Why or why not?

- What is the fastest you have gone in a car?

- Do you think cars are safe?

- What are some of the advantages and disadvantages of driving versus public transportation?

- What do you think cars will be like in the future?

- Do people drive well in your country?

- Would you like to drive an F-1 race car?

- Do you think the use of cars will increase or decrease in the future? Why?

Challenges

- What is a challenge you have faced?

- There are many amazing challenges to try: Visiting all of the continents, swimming in all of the oceans of the world, or climbing Everest. Can you think of some more interesting challenges that a person can do?

- What kind of challenge would you like to try?

- Do you have any heroes that have done something amazing?

- Challenges don't have to be amazing. What are some normal challenges people face?

- Some people think that facing challenges improves a person. Do you agree or disagree?

- Can you think of a friend who overcame a challenge?

- What are some challenges you think the next generation will face?

- Should people make their children have easy lives with few challenges or make sure their children face challenges?

- What is the next challenge in your life you want to overcome?

Change

- Are you someone who likes change?

- In what ways have you changed since you were in junior high school?

- How do you think you will change in the future?

- Which political party in your country is most likely to make big changes? Is that a good or bad thing?

- "The only thing constant is change." Do you agree with this statement? Explain.

- What are the biggest changes in the world you have seen since you were a child?

- What is the biggest change most people experience in their lives?

- Is change good or bad for a person's mental health?

- What is the most positive change you have experienced in your life?

- "You are the same person you were five years ago except for the books you have read, the people you have met, and the places you have traveled." Do you think this quote is accurate?

Charity

- Do you give to charity or volunteer?

- What do you think are some important charities people should give to?

- Do you know of any bizarre charities?

- Do you give money to homeless people? Do you think people should give money to homeless people?

- Who do you think needs charity the most?

- How much do you think governments should give to help other countries?

- Should rich people and corporations be forced to give to charity?

- Do you think there are charities that are scams?

- Does your country have a holiday when it is traditional to help out people in your community? If not, should there be a holiday like that?

- Do you think it is better to give time or money?

Choices

- Would you rather live in your own country or live abroad?

- Would you rather be smart or beautiful/handsome?

- Would you rather be poor and happy or rich and unhappy?

- Would you rather marry someone plain with a good personality or someone beautiful without much personality?

- If war broke out in your country would you rather flee the country or fight?

- Would you rather be rich or famous?

- If you had to lose one of your senses (sight, smell, hearing, touch, taste) which would you rather lose?

- Would you rather marry a rich celebrity or a rich CEO?

- Would you rather have a brand new Mac or PC?

- Would you rather take a trip to a new country or get a new TV?

Cities

- Do you like cities or the country side? Which is better and why?

- You can make one change to your city. What will you change?

- What are some of the most famous cities in the world? What makes them famous?

- Why do you think that humans started living in cities?

- What will cities be like 50 years from now? Think about how these will change: Transportation, pollution, crime, advertising, buildings, work, shopping, and nightlife.

- Do you think that we will still live in cities 100 years from now?

- What city would you like to visit?

- What city is best known for fashion? How about technology? Art? Industry? Tourism?

- What makes a city great to live in?

- Are cities good for the environment or bad for the environment?

Cleanliness

- How clean is too clean?

- How dirty is too dirty?

- How can bacteria help humans?

- If you drop food on the floor, do you pick it up, blow it off/dust it off, and eat it?

- What is the dirtiest job?

- How often do you wash your hands with soap?

- What is the grossest thing you have seen someone do?

- Did your mom let you get dirty when you were a child?

- What is the dirtiest you have ever been?

- How often do you clean your house or room?

- Do you do the dishes right after eating? How long do you let the dirty dishes sit without washing them?

- Do you know anyone who is VERY concerned about germs and cleanliness?

Cloning

- Do you know how scientists clone animals? What is the process?

- Do you think scientists should be allowed to clone people?

- Would you want to have a clone of yourself?

- What problems could cloning people solve?

- Could cloning people lead to problems? What kinds of problems?

- If we could clone dinosaurs and bring them back to life, would you want to?

- How about cloning ancient humans, like Neanderthals or the early Homo sapiens? Would you want to clone ancient humans?

- Should we clone famous people like Albert Einstein or Leonardo Da Vinci? Do you think they would be as successful if they were brought back as clones?

- How can cloning animals help science?

- What do you think cloning will be like in the future? Will cloning stop or expand?

Collectibles

- Do you collect anything now? How about when you were a child?

- Did your parents collect anything as you were growing up?

- What is the strangest thing you have heard of people collecting?

- What do you think about hoarders who collect almost everything (old newspapers, hair, ketchup packets, etc.) and store it in their house?

- What things can you collect that increase in value over time?

- Is there anything you want to start collecting?

- Are collectibles a good investment?

- What are some things that are new now that might be worth collecting?

- Did you play any collectible card games when you were a child?

- Who has a collection that you are jealous of?

- Should famous art collections be allowed to be kept in private homes or should they be controlled by governments?

Color

- What is your favorite color?

- Is color important to you?

- Does color affect your emotions?

- Imagine being in a room where everything is dark blue, how would you feel?

- What if the room was red? Black? Yellow? Pink?

- Why do you think colors affect humans so much?

- Do you think that certain colors are only for boys or only for girls?

- Which colors do guys usually like more? How about girls? Why do you think there is a difference?

- If you HAD to change your hair color, what color would you change it to?

- Most electronics are black, silver or white. Why do you think this is? Do you think we will have more colorful electronics in the future?

- Can you think of some examples of colors being used as camouflage in daily life?

Communication

- How is communication changing between people?

- Talking to strangers used to be common. Do you think we should talk to people we don't know?

- How often do you start up a conversation with people you don't know?

- Think about how your grandmother talks with people. Is it the same as how you talk to people?

- How will people communicate in the future?

- How have smart phones changed communication?

- Name at least ten forms of communication.

- Do you think people can communicate with ghosts and spirits?

- How has communication changed through human history?

- What is the most basic form of communication?

Computers

- Do you know anything about the history of computers?

- Do you own a computer? What do you use it for?

- Think about smart-phones. Do you consider them computers? Why or why not?

- Computers are starting to be built into new houses and apartments. Would you like a computer to control your house for you?

- Do you think the invention and rise of computers has been a good thing or a bad thing? Why?

- Talk about the first computer you ever used.

- What will be the future of computers?

- Do you think people rely too much on computers?

- Do you think computers will ever be able to think for themselves or have "real" intelligence?

- What do you think will happen if computers become self-aware?

- Talk about the differences between how you use a computer and how children use a computer.

Conspiracies and Cover Ups

- What are some famous real conspiracies or cover ups?

- What are some common conspiracy theories? Do you think they will be proven right or proven wrong?

- Do you think that newspapers sometimes cover up events?

- How often do politicians in your country get in trouble because of cover ups?

- Do you think it's possible for global conspiracies to exist?

- Whose job is it to uncover conspiracies and expose cover ups?

- How open should governments be? Do governments need some secrecy?

- Are you a suspicious or trusting person?

- What are some secret societies you have heard of? Do you think they really exist?

- When are secrets a good thing?

Cooking

- How often do you cook?

- How good are you at cooking?

- What are some things that you can cook?

- What dish or food are you best at cooking?

- Do you think you can cook better than your mother?

- Who is a better cook, your mother or your grandmother?

- Are cooking shows popular in your country? Do you watch any cooking shows?

- What is the hardest thing to cook?

- What are some of the advantages of cooking your meals at home? How about the disadvantages?

- If you had your own personal chef, what meal would you ask for most?

- How hard is it to become a chef? What do you have to do to become a chef?

Corruption

- Is there a lot of corruption in your country?

- What businesses have the most corruption in your country?

- What are some problems with corruption in the political system of your country?

- Do you think corruption will always be a part of business and politics?

- What recent corruption scandal was in the news?

- Who is the most corrupt politician or businessperson you know of?

- What is the best way to fight corruption in business and politics?

- Is corruption ever justified?

- Can a corrupt organization ever be more efficient than a less corrupt organization if they are about the same size and in the same industry?

- If you were in a position of power, do you think you would be corrupt?

Creativity

- Are you a creative person?

- Which art medium is the most creative? (Painting, music, film, photography, etc.)

- Who is the most creative person you know?

- Are creative people more emotional?

- What do you do that is creative?

- How important is creativity for success in business?

- Do you think a person can train themselves to be creative? If so, how?

- Who were some of the most creative people in the last 50 years?

- How does technology help creativity? Can technology hurt creativity?

- Do you wish you were more creative? Why?

- Are people born creative or do they become creative? Could we genetically engineer people to be more creative?

Crime

- Is shoplifting common in your country?

- What do you think the most common crime in your country is?

- Should police in your country be stricter or less strict?

- Is your country a safe country?

- Have you ever seen a crime? (Don't talk about it if it's too upsetting for you.)

- Do you think criminals can change their behavior?

- What type of person shoplifts and what kinds of things do they steal?

- Does your country have a big mafia?

- Have you ever met someone from the mafia?

- Can you tell if a kid will grow up to be a criminal?

Customs

- Have you ever traveled abroad? If you have, where did you go and what was it like? What customs were different from your country's customs? If you haven't, would you like to go to abroad? Where would you like to go and what do you think it will be like?

- Do you think it is important to follow a country's customs when you visit there?

- What are some of the most important customs of your country? How about the customs of a country near your country? How about America or Australia?

- Do you follow all of your country's traditional customs?

- What are some strange foreign customs that you have heard of?

- Are there any customs in your country visitors might find strange?

- How do people greet each other in your country? Has it changed from the past?

- Do you enjoy learning about other countries' customs?

- What are some customs in your country that people should follow when they are eating? Do you think other countries have the same custom?

- What are some interesting wedding customs in your country?

Dating

- Where is the best place in your city to take a date?

- What can you do if you want to save money and go on a date?

- How common are blind dates in your country?

- Do most blind dates go well? If not, why not?

- What is the best way to meet boyfriends or girlfriends?

- Describe your ideal date.

- What was the worst/best date that you have ever been on?

- When a boy and a girl go on a date, which should pay?

- How many people should you date before getting married?

- What do you think of double dates?

Disabilities

- How does the government in your country help disabled people?

- What are some common disabilities?

- How do you think disabled people feel when people pity them?

- Are you comfortable around disabled people?

- What is the best thing we can do to help disabled people?

- Do you know anyone who is disabled?

- Do you think your country's government does enough to help disabled people?

- In your opinion, what are the worst disabilities?

- How are disabilities viewed in your country?

- What kinds of disabilities do people develop as they grow older?

Dreaming

- How often do you dream?

- Do you dream in color or black and white?

- Have you ever had a flying dream?

- Have you ever been falling in a dream and just when you are about to hit the ground you wake up?

- Do you think dreams have meanings?

- Do you think dreams can tell the future?

- Have you ever been dreaming and woken up and couldn't move?

- What was the best or worst dream you can remember? Don't share your dream if it's too personal or too intense.

- Why do we forget dreams so quickly?

- Have you ever kept a dream journal?

- Why do we dream? What is the purpose of dreams?

- Do you think animals dream, too? What kind of dreams do you think they have?

- What does your country's culture traditionally believe about dreams?

- Have you ever had déjà vue?

Drugs

- What illegal drugs can you name?

- What are some drugs that used to be legal but aren't anymore?

- Why are some dangerous drugs legal (alcohol, nicotine, caffeine, etc.), but other safer drugs are illegal? Do you use any legal drugs?

- Do you think your country has a drug problem?

- Most illegal drugs started out as medicine. What medicine might be made illegal in the future?

- What would happen if all illegal drugs were legalized?

- Are there any illegal drugs you think should be made legal? How about drugs that are legal but should be illegal?

- Where do most illegal drugs come from?

- Why do people start taking illegal drugs?

- Is addiction to drugs a disease or a crime?

Eating Habits

- Talk about what you have eaten today.

- What is the unhealthiest food you can think of?

- What do people need to eat more of?

- Do you usually eat healthy food?

- What are some different types of diets you have heard of?

- Do you think your parents ate healthier food at your age than you do? How about your grandparents?

- Do you eat a lot of small portions or a few large portions of food each day?

- Do you think people from your country usually eat healthy food?

- What are some things about your eating habits you want to change?

- Do you think that organic food is much better than normal food or are they about the same?

- Why is organic food so much more expensive?

- What is traditional food in your country like? Is it healthy?

- Do you think that a person's eating habits affect how long they will live?

Electric Cars

- Would you ever drive an electric car?

- What are some of the benefits and disadvantages of electric cars?

- When do you think the first electric car was made?

- What technology needs to be improved to make electric cars more popular?

- Are electric cars really environmentally friendly if the electricity to charge them comes from coal power plants?

- Do you think electric cars, hydrogen cars, or something totally different will be the future of automobiles?

- How long does it take to charge an electric car?

- Which country do you think is trying the hardest to make electric cars popular?

- Do you think electric cars are popular in your country? Why or why not?

- Do you think electric planes will become popular soon?

Email

- How often do you send emails?

- How many email accounts do you have/need?

- What email provider do you use?

- How much of the email that you receive is spam?

- Have you ever hand-written a letter and sent it to someone? If no, why not? If yes, how often do you send letters?

- Have you ever pressed "send" and then wished you hadn't?

- If you could secretly view anyone's email, whose email would you spy on?

- What was the best email you have ever received?

- What can happen if someone steals your email password?

- Have you ever gotten a computer virus from email?

Empathy

- How much empathy do you feel towards other people?

- Do you think it's possible to be too empathetic?

- Why might it be bad/good for a doctor to have a lot of empathy?

- In what other jobs is empathy very important?

- Who is the most empathetic person you know?

- When is it bad to have empathy?

- Why do you think humans feel empathy? Do you think animals can feel empathy?

- Do you think that people are born with empathy or are they taught it?

- If you see a homeless person on the street asking for money, what is the first thing you think about them?

- Are you good at knowing when something is wrong with a coworker or family member?

- What does the idiom "I feel your pain" mean? Have you ever felt some else's pain?

Entrepreneurs

- What are four pros and four cons of being an entrepreneur?

- Do you know any entrepreneurs?

- Does your country have a lot of entrepreneurs? Why do you think so?

- What is the most profitable type of business to open in your country?

- Should a restaurant open where there are no restaurants or lots of restaurants?

- In your country, is it better for a restaurant or café to be unique or familiar?

- How are businesses today different from businesses in the past?

- What must a company do or have to be successful?

- Are people born entrepreneurs or are they made?

- What traits make someone a good entrepreneur?

- Would you like to open your own business? Why or why not?

Environmental Problems

- What are some of the most serious environmental problems?

- What are ten things individuals can do to help the environment?

- What are five things governments can do to help the environment?

- What is your opinion on climate change?

- Which countries cause the most pollution?

- How will our children be affected by climate change?

- What kinds of technologies do you know of that might help stop environmental problems?

- Are corporations responsible for helping the environment?

- What are some things that corporations can do to help the environment?

- What are some local environmental problems you have noticed?

- Do you think houses will be more environmentally friendly in the future?

- Where will we get our energy when we run out of oil?

- How will India and China affect the environment in the future?

- What will happen if we keep polluting the environment?

- Will the climate keep changing or go back to normal?

Ethics

- Do you consider yourself to be an ethical person?

- Have you ever found a lost smart phone? What did you do? If you haven't, what do you think you would do?

- Would you risk your life to save another person?

- Would you jump into a deep river to save a drowning animal?

- What should a person do if they find a wallet? What do people usually do? What would you do?

- What are some ethical dilemmas you have faced?

- Is stealing ALWAYS wrong? When is it right to steal?

- If you could save ten people by killing one person, would you?

- How often do you lie? When is it okay to lie?

- What makes a person act ethically or unethically?

- If you saw a pickpocket stealing someone's wallet what would you do?

- Should poor people be punished for stealing if they are stealing to feed their family?

Facts and Statistics

- What do you think about these facts and statistics:

    An office desk has 400 times more bacteria than a toilet.

    Ten percent of all human beings ever born are alive at this very moment.

    Most lipstick contains fish scales.

    You have more bacteria cells in your body than human cells.

- What are some interesting statistics you know of?

- What do you think the saying "Numbers don't lie" means?

- What are some of the problems with statistics?

- Do you agree that "42.7% of statistics are made up on the spot"?

- What separates a fact from an opinion?

- Have you ever taken a survey? What was it for?

- Are the results from surveys an accurate form of statistics?

- Have you ever made up a statistic to make what you were saying more trustworthy?

- Do you trust statistics when you hear them?

Family

- How do members of a family support each other?

- Who do you think has the most power in the family? Why?

- Are good family members or good friends more important? Why?

- How close are you to your extended family? (Cousins, aunts, uncles, etc.)

- What do you think of people who marry and decide not to have children?

- How do you think western culture families and eastern culture families differ?

- What do you think is the most important thing to make a happy family?

- Is it better for mothers to stay at home with their kids or go to work to earn more money for the family?

- Many families send their children to private institutes or daycares for most of the day. Is this good or bad?

- How do you define the word "home"? Is it where you live, where your family lives, or where you grew up?

- When married people talk about having children they talk about "starting a family". Can two married people be a family if they don't have kids?

- How do you think family life is changing in your country? (Example: wife working, husband cleaning, etc.) Is this change good or bad?

- What do you think of gay marriage?

- Is spanking or hitting a good way to discipline children? Why or why not?

Family Values

- What values will you pass on to your children?

- Do you think society is losing its values?

- How have values changed in society?

- What is a value other people think is very important that you don't think is important?

- What values did your parents pass on to you?

- Are there any values that your parents tried to make you follow but you weren't good at following?

- How do values hold a society together?

- Some people say that poorer societies have stronger values than richer countries. Do you agree?

- What traditional values are not important or not necessary now?

- How do you feel when you see someone not following the values you were brought up with?

Fashion

- Would you like to be a fashion model? What are their lives like?

- Could you date someone if they had a terrible sense of fashion?

- Which country or city is the most fashionable in the world?

- Is fashion important or not important? Why or why not?

- Do you prefer functional or fashionable clothing?

- What do you think of the fashion industry?

- How does fashion affect people's lives?

- What are some of the silliest fashions you have seen?

- Do you think fashions changed as quickly in the past as today? Why or why not?

- If you were a fashion designer, what kind of clothes would you design?

Fast Food

- What is your least favorite fast food restaurant? Why?

- Does fast food taste good or bad? Why?

- Why is fast food so popular?

- How often do you eat fast food? What do you usually eat? Where?

- What is a fast food that people think is healthy but really isn't?

- Do you know anyone who has worked at a fast food restaurant? How did they like it?

- How has fast food changed in your country?

- How is your country's fast food different from other countries' fast food?

- Can you think of any healthy fast food?

- How would you define "fast food"?

First Impressions

- When you look at someone, what makes you think they are dangerous, greedy, intelligent, kind, not smart, crazy, or generous?

- Do you like to meet new people or do you prefer to hang out with people you already know?

- When and where did you meet most of your friends for the first time?

- Have you met someone you hated right away even though you didn't know them?

- When are the most important times to make a good first impression?

- What are the best ways to make a good first impression?

- Do you make first impressions based on what people wear?

- What kind of impression are you trying to make with your clothes?

- Do you try to make a different first impression now than you did in high school?

- Have you ever tried to make a great first impression but completely messed it up?

- In what jobs do people have to make very quick decisions based on first impressions?

The Five Senses

- What is your favorite sense? Why is it your favorite?

- If you had to lose one sense, which would it be?

- Do you think we have any other senses? (i.e., when you can feel that someone is staring at you even if you can't see them or ESP)

- Which sense would you like to improve, if possible?

- What is the most beautiful thing to see?

- What is the most wonderful smell?

- What is the best taste?

- What is the greatest sound?

- What is the most wonderful thing to touch?

- Which of your senses is the most sensitive?

- Which of your senses is the least sensitive?

Food

- What kinds of food did you eat when you were a child? Do you eat the same things now?

- What is the best food to eat when you are sick?

- What is your favorite food that your mother/father cooks?

- How often do you eat out?

- If you could have any food right now, what would it be?

- How would you describe your country's food?

- What is your favorite food? What's in it? Why is it your favorite?

- What is your favorite foreign food? How is it different from your country's cuisine?

- Where is the best place to eat in your town? Why is it so good?

- Do you eat a healthy diet? Why or why not?

- What could you do to improve your diet?

- Have you ever gone on a diet to improve your health or lose weight? How well did it work?

- Do you eat different foods depending on the season or weather? Give some examples.

- What kinds of food can you cook? Would you like to learn how to cook more types of food?

Free Time

- What are some things you like to do in your free time?

- Do you have more free time now or when you were a kid?

- What would you do if you had more free time?

- Is there such a thing as too much free time?

- How do free time activities differ now compared with the past?

- Do you think people had more or less free time in the past?

- What is the most worthwhile thing a person can do with their free time?

- What does the idiom "Time is money" mean? Do you agree with it?

- Is there something you wish you could do with your free time but can't?

- Do you think a four day work week would be a good idea?

Friendship

- Do you prefer to have many friends or just a few that are close?

- What are the benefits of having just a few close friends? How about the benefits of having many friends?

- Describe your best friend.

- Are you close friends with anyone who you knew in elementary school?

- Why do people need friends? What can happen if a person has no friends?

- What is the biggest thing you have done to help a friend?

- Do you have any friends who would risk their life to save you?

- Would you risk your life to save a friend? How about a stranger?

- What kind of qualities do you look for in a friend?

- What is the best way to make new friends? Do you like making new friends?

- Do you think sites like Facebook are good for friendships or do they stop people from becoming close?

- How did you meet your best friend?

Fruits and Vegetables

- What fruits are most popular in your country?

- What is your favorite fruit? Why?

- Have you ever thought about becoming a vegetarian? Do you know anyone who is a vegetarian?

- What is your favorite vegetarian dish?

- Did you like vegetables when you were a child?

- Do you eat fruit or baked goods for dessert?

- What is the best vegetable or fruit for a quick snack?

- Where do you go to buy your fruits and vegetables?

- How often do you eat fruit?

- Do you eat vegetables at every meal?

- Are organic vegetables and fruits actually better?

Future

- Will humans ever meet aliens? What will the meeting be like?

- What kind sci-fi movie will the future be like?

- Will science find a solution to the environmental problems we have? What kind of solution will it be?

- Will computers ever take over the world?

- Will we be able to add machines to most of our body to improve it in the future?

- When will humans live on another planet?

- How will electronics be different in the future?

- How will medicine and health care change in the future?

- How do you think you will change in the future?

- Where will you be and what will you be doing in ten years?

- What is something that will happen in the future that you are looking forward to?

- How will you change the world?

Games

- How many genres of video games can you name?

- How are some of these genres unique and different from the others?

- Choose one or two examples of games or video games. What are their rules?

- What kinds of games are popular now?

- What were some games that were popular in the past?

- What makes a good game?

- Are games good for you or bad for you?

- Are games in the present better or worse than games in the past?

- What is your favorite way to play games (cards, console, computer, mobile, sports)?

- Compare games your parents played with games you like to play.

Getting a Job

- What is the best way to find a job?

- What do you think are the five most common questions asked at a job interview?

- What are some things you should do for a job interview? How about things you shouldn't do?

- How is the job market in your country? Is it easy or difficult to get a job?

- How many jobs have you had? What were the interviews like?

- If you were going to change jobs or try to get a job, what kind of job would you want to apply for?

- How should a person dress when they go for a job interview?

- How should you act when you are in a job interview? Confident? Polite? Humble?

- What are resumes like in your country? What information do employers want to know?

- What are some good things to have on your resume?

Glasses and Contacts

- Do you wear glasses or contacts? If so, when did you start wearing them?

- Do you think that people today have worse eyesight than in the past? Why or why not?

- Do you know of anyone who has had corrective eye surgery? Were they happy with the results?

- What do you think about people wearing glasses they don't need, just for fashion?

- People often think that glasses make people look smart. Why do you think this is?

- What do you think about contact lenses that change the color of someone's eyes?

- What types of glasses are in fashion now?

- How will technology change glasses?

- In developing countries glasses can sometime be hard to get. How can that problem be fixed?

- Do you think that in the future no one will wear glasses?

Golf

- Have you ever played golf on a real golf course?

- Have you ever been to a driving range?

- Does your country have putt putt/miniature golf?

- What do you think about golf being in the Olympics?

- Have you ever watched golf on TV? What did you think of it? (e.g., boring, exciting, interesting, etc.)

- Is playing golf a part of doing business in your country?

- How many famous golfers do you know?

- Do you think golf is a rich person's game or is it open to everyone?

- Who in your family loves golf the most?

- What would make golf more exciting to play or watch?

Habits

- What are some things you do every day?

- What are some good habits you have?

- Do you have any bad habits? Can your partner or group give you any advice for your bad habits?

- What is something you should do every day but don't?

- What are some activities you like to do?

- How much exercise do you get every week?

- What is a successful life? What habits should you have to have a successful life?

- What three habits will improve your life?

- What are some habits that can improve your English ability?

- What is something you do about once a week, month or year?

Having Children

- How does having children change someone's life?

- What kinds of things do people have to give up when they have children?

- What are some of the benefits of having children?

- What is the perfect number of children a family should have?

- Do you think it is better to have children when you are older or younger?

- Do you want to have children? If not, why not? Have you told your parents about your decision? What do they think about it? If so, when do you want to have children and how many do you want to have? Do you want your first child to be a boy or a girl? Why?

- Most families in wealthy countries are having less and less children. Is this a good thing or a bad thing? Why?

- How do children who have no brothers or sisters act?

- Do you agree with the saying "Children should be seen and not heard"? Why do you agree or disagree?

- What age did women start having children sixty years ago? How about now?

- Do you like seeing pictures of other people's babies?

- What are the best and worst things about having children?

Health

- What is the most important thing to do to stay healthy?

- What do you think the worst disease to have would be?

- Do you consider yourself to be healthy? Why?

- How often do you exercise?

- What is your diet like? Do you eat mostly fruits and vegetables?

- What do you think about the health care system in your country? How could it be improved?

- People are living longer and longer thanks to medicine. How long would you like to live? How about forever?

- Are there any diseases that you think humans could eliminate if we tried?

- Where do you think the future of medicine will be? Genetics? Cybernetics? Chemistry?

- Would you like to get your genome sequenced?

- If you could find out that you were at risk to get a certain disease, would you want to know?

History

- How much do you know about your country's history?

- Who is your favorite person from history?

- What historical event had the most impact on the world?

- Should history be taught more, or less, in schools?

- George Santayana said, "Those who cannot remember the past are condemned to repeat it." Do you agree?

- Is it more important to teach world history or your native country's history?

- What is the most interesting period of history?

- What are some of your favorite historical movies?

- Who is your country's most famous historical figure?

- What historical event should be made into a movie?

Hobbies

- What are some of your hobbies?

- How and when did you start your hobby?

- Is it important for people to have hobbies?

- What are some strange hobbies you have heard of?

- What kind of new hobby would you like to try?

- Do you think that some hobbies are just for girls and some are just for boys?

- What are some of your family members' hobbies?

- What are some hobbies that improve a person's life?

- Do you know of anyone whose hobby is out of control and has gone too far?

- What hobbies are based on certain seasons?

Holidays

- What is your favorite holiday? Has your favorite holiday changed since you were a kid?

- On what holiday do people in your country eat a lot of food?

- Do you give gifts on any holidays?

- What foreign holidays do you know about?

- What is the strangest holiday or festival you have heard of?

- Do you think that all countries have similar holidays?

- Talk about your best memory from a holiday.

- Are there any holidays that you really don't like?

- Do you think your country should have more or less holidays? Why?

- Does your country have parades during holidays? Have you ever been to a parade?

- What is the most important holiday?

Homes

- Is your home clean? Are you a very organized person?

- Do you have a lot of decorations in your home or is it bare?

- Are you happy with the size of your home?

- What is your favorite appliance, electronic device, or piece of furniture in your home?

- If you had $3,000 to improve your home, what would you spend it on?

- Do you agree with the saying "Wherever I lay my head is home"?

- How is your home different from your childhood home?

- What would you say the decoration style of your home is?

- What would your ideal house or apartment look like?

- What do you do to maintain your home?

- What household chores do you hate doing?

Hotels

- Which do you prefer to stay in when you travel? Hotels, hostels, or another type of place? Why?

- What are the best and worst things about staying in hotels?

- Have you ever been to a really disgusting hotel? Did you stay or leave?

- Do you feel comfortable when you are staying at a hotel?

- Have you ever ordered room service?

- What are the best alternatives to staying at a hotel?

- Do you have any interesting stories about staying somewhere other than your house, like a hotel or hostel?

- Are hotels common in your country? If not, where do people stay when they travel?

- What is the nicest hotel you have stayed at?

- What would it be like to work in a hotel as a cleaning person or front desk staff?

- Have you ever eaten anything out of the minibar (the refrigerator with snacks and drinks)? Was it expensive?

Human Wonders

- How many of the seven ancient wonders can you name? How many are left?

- 100 million votes were cast for the new human wonders of the world. The new seven wonders are:

  Chichén Itzá, Mexico / Christ the Redeemer, Brazil / the Great Wall, China / Machu Picchu, Peru / Petra, Jordan / the Roman Colosseum, Italy / the Taj Mahal, India.

- Have you been to any of them or do you know someone who has been to one of the new Seven Wonders of the World??

- What do you know about each one?

- Which ones would you like to go to?

- Why do you think people voted for these wonders?

- Are there any you would add to this list of human made wonders?

- Can you think of any wonders made in the last 50 years?

- What are some of the human made wonders in your country?

- If you could build another wonder of the world, what would it be?

- Do you think it is a good idea for governments to fund "wonders" for their countries? Why or why not?

- Which would you prefer to see, human wonders or natural wonders? Why?

Humor

- What are some funny TV shows you enjoy?

- Do you have any favorite comedians? Why are they so funny?

- What kind of humor do you find the most funny?

- Do your friends think you are funny?

- Do you know any jokes? If you do, tell a few of them.

- Do you think that different cultures have different senses of humor?

- What are some things that are funny across all cultures?

- What is the funniest thing you have seen or heard this week?

- What do you think the best medium (TV, books, music, etc.) for humor is?

- Do you think that animals find things funny?

Idols

- Who are the most popular singers or groups in your country?

- What are some crazy examples of fans showing their love that you have heard of?

- When do fans go too far?

- Are there any groups that you are a huge fan of?

- What were some of the groups that you really loved when you were younger?

- Besides singers and groups, who else is idolized?

- Is it natural to idolize famous people? Why?

- Do you want to be famous? Why or why not?

- Why do teenagers idolize famous people more than other age groups?

- Do you feel sorry for famous people being bothered by paparazzi or do you think it is part of their job?

Immigration

- When is immigration helpful to a country and when is it harmful?

- Do you think your country needs more or less immigrants?

- What nationalities are most immigrants who come to your country?

- What would happen if we erased all country borders and let people live wherever they wanted? Would it be a good or bad thing? Why?

- Does your country have strict immigration laws? Should the laws be less strict or stricter?

- What should immigrants know before they can become citizens?

- What is the best method to slow or stop immigration? Can immigration ever be completely stopped?

- Do you think immigrants to a country work harder than people born in that country? Why or why not?

- Do you have any friends or family who are immigrants? How does that affect your view of immigration?

- How do immigrants help a country's economy?

Individuality

- What makes you unique?

- Is it okay to look different from other people or should you look the same as other people?

- What do you think when you see someone who looks very different?

- If you went to a job interview with green hair, what do you think would happen?

- If you see someone with a lot of tattoos, what do you think of them?

- Have you ever felt like a square peg in a round hole?

- What are some things you do to blend in?

- If you had to do one crazy thing to your appearance what would you do?

- If you got a tattoo, what would it be?

- Is everyone unique or are all humans basically the same?

Intelligence

- Can intelligence be measured? If so, what is the best way to measure it? If not, why not?

- What is the most intelligent animal?

- Do you think that intelligence is only based on genetics or can a child's environment boost intelligence?

- How intelligent do you think you are?

- Why are very intelligent children born to parents who are not very intelligent?

- Some people say that there are many geniuses born around the world but they can't reach their full potential because they live in a poor country. Do you agree?

- What separates a person from being very intelligent and being a genius?

- Do you think that we can create artificial intelligence?

- If scientists could put a chip in your head that would make you twice as intelligent, would you have the surgery done?

- Very intelligent people are often not very good at being social, why do you think this is?

The Internet

- How much time do you spend on the internet?

- What are some of the benefits of the internet?

- What are some of the dangers of the internet?

- How much time should children spend on the internet?

- How has the internet changed the world?

- What will the internet be like in ten years?

- Which social networks are you a part of?

- When did you get your first email address?

- How often do you communicate through email versus social networks?

- What website do you spend the most time on?

- If you could recommend just one website, what would it be?

Investing

- Do you think it is better to save money or invest money? Why?

- Do you think that investing in the stock market is safe?

- Compare the advantages and disadvantages of investing in the stock market versus investing in real estate.

- What are some more ways people can invest their money?

- Do you think that education is an investment?

- Who is the richest person in your country? How did they make their money?

- What is the best thing you can invest money in?

- When it comes to investing are you a risk taker or do you play it safe?

- What are some of the benefits and disadvantages of investing in individual stocks versus mutual funds?

- How do you feel about investment banks who invest your money for you?

- What is the worst investment someone can make?

Jobs

- What are some of the worst jobs you can think of?

- What are some of the best jobs you can think of?

- How long do you want to work?

- Is it better to be a boss or an employee? Why?

- What would be the most satisfying job for you?

- What is one of the most exciting jobs you can think of? How about one of the most boring jobs?

- What kind of job do you want to get in the future? What kind of tasks will you have to do?

- Do you think a person's job determines who they are?

- What is the most dangerous job?

- How difficult is it to get a job in your country?

- What company is the best to work for?

Languages

- Which languages are the most difficult to learn?

- Which languages are the easiest to learn?

- How many languages can you speak?

- Does one of your family members or friends speak a lot of languages?

- What is the angriest sounding language?

- What do you think the oldest language is?

- How many languages can you say "hello" in?

- What do you know about the Esperanto language?

- What is the most romantic sounding language?

- Should languages be preserved? Why or why not? What is the best way to preserve languages?

Learning English

- Why are you learning English?

- Do you enjoy learning English?

- How much would you pay for a pill that instantly allows you to speak perfect English?

- What is most difficult about learning English for you? What is easiest about learning English?

- What is the best way to improve your speaking skill?

- What is the best way to improve your listening, reading, and writing skills?

- Are you nervous about making mistakes while speaking English?

- How has learning English improved your life?

- Should English be taught in public schools? If so, how should it be taught?

- English is often used as a common language between two people who speak different languages. Is there a language that would be better to use as a common language?

Love

- Do you believe that love can be understood by looking at the brain and chemicals?

- How is attraction different than love?

- Why do you think some people fall out of love?

- What is the most romantic movie you know of?

- In public, how much affection is too much?

- How is showing love different now from in the past?

- In all cultures there are famous love stories (i.e., Romeo and Juliet). What is a famous love story in your country?

- When you see a couple, how do you know they are in love?

- Do you believe in love at first sight?

- What do you think of Valentine's Day?

- Think of two different cultures. How do those cultures express love differently?

- Why are most songs about love?

Luck

- Do you consider yourself to be lucky or unlucky?

- Do you have any good luck charms?

- Does your country have any superstitions about bad luck? For example, what causes bad luck?

- What about good luck? How can someone improve their luck?

- Do you think some people are just born lucky?

- What are some idioms about luck in your country?

- Do you know of anyone who has a lot of good luck? How about someone who is really unlucky?

- Do you believe in luck or do you think it's all just chance?

- Some people believe that the harder you work, the luckier you are. Do you agree or disagree?

- Why do you think so many athletes have good luck rituals?

Luxury Items

- What is one luxury item you really want to have?

- Do developed countries focus too much on luxury items?

- What do you think is the most popular luxury item in your country? Who is it made by?

- What is the craziest example of a luxury item you have heard of?

- Have you ever been jealous that someone had something you didn't?

- Do you think that luxury goods make people happy? Why or why not?

- What do you think expensive perfume is made from?

- What is something that you can spend money on that will make you happy? How long will it make you happy for?

- Who are the best electronics made by?

- Do brand name prices mean great quality?

- Which types of products must have brand names if you are going to buy them?

- How often do you spend money on things you know you shouldn't? What kind of things do you buy?

- Who are the most expensive cars made by?

- Are rich people really happier?

Manners

- What are some examples of bad manners on the bus?

- What are some examples of good manners on the subway?

- What are some examples of bad manners that you HATE?

- Do you think people are more polite or less polite now than in the past?

- Do you know someone who is often rude?

- Can you think of some examples of how manners have changed in your country?

- How are manners different in other countries?

- How important is it to be polite to older people even though they are often rude?

- What is something that isn't considered rude but should be?

- When someone is rude in a public place, do you say something or try to ignore the person?

Marriage

- What makes a happy marriage?

- How does/did the idea of getting married make you feel? Excited? Scared? Happy? Nervous?

- What advice did your parents give you about getting married?

- Some people say that marriage is outdated (too old-fashioned and not needed). Do you agree or disagree?

- Describe your perfect spouse.

- What do you think married life will be like? If you are married, what is married life like?

- When do you plan on getting married? If you are already married, when did you get married?

- What do you want your wedding to be like? If you are already married, what was your wedding like?

- What are some wedding traditions in your country?

- What do you think of arranged marriages?

- What age is too young to get married?

- Why do people get married?

Massage

- How is massage viewed in your country? How common is it?

- How are masseuses and masseurs viewed in your country? Are they well respected?

- Does your country have a long history of massages or is massage somewhat new to your country?

- What types of massage are popular in your country?

- When was the last time you got a professional massage? How about a nonprofessional massage?

- Are massage chairs popular in your country?

- Have you tried many different types of massage?

- Have you ever used a massage chair or some other massage device? How was it?

- Some massage chairs cost thousands of dollars. Do you think expensive massage chairs are worth the price?

- Can a massage chair ever be as good as a human masseuse or masseur? What are the pros and cons of a massage chair versus a human masseuse or masseur?

- What do you think the future of massage will be?

The Media

- Where do most people in your country get their news?

- Does the media in your country report the whole truth, mostly truth, or mostly lies?

- How has the internet changed the news in your country?

- Who has the most control over the media in your country?

- How does the media help create a healthy society?

- Should the media just report the facts or should the media interpret the facts?

- Can you think of a politician who used the media in a successful way? How about a politician who was destroyed by the media?

- Should the media show graphic violence? Why or why not?

- How has the media changed in your country during the last 20 years?

- What is the most fair and balanced media outlet in your country?

Medicine

- Has medicine ever saved your life?

- What disease will be cured next by advances in medicine?

- Do you think there will ever be a cure for aging?

- How could modern medicine be improved?

- Who should pay for medicine when a person gets sick? The government, the sick person, or their workplace?

- What do you think was the most important medicine ever discovered?

- What do you think about gene therapy as medicine?

- What will be the future of medicine?

- What do you think of people who refuse to take modern medicine and will only use natural remedies?

- Is there any medicine you can think of that has done more harm than good?

Meeting New People

- If you don't know your group very well, ask them some questions to get to know them.

- Do you like meeting new people? Why or why not?

- What are some things that you usually talk about when you meet a new person?

- If you see a handsome boy/beautiful girl that you want to get to know, what is the best way to approach them?

- Why don't strangers talk to each other as often as they used to?

- Have you ever had a stranger come up and start talking to you? How did you respond?

- Do you know any funny "pick-up lines"?

- Do you think that some people are destined to meet?

- Where is the best place to meet new people?

- Have you ever met someone you hated right after meeting them?

Memory

- How good is your memory?

- What is the best memory you have?

- Who was your most memorable teacher? (Bad or good)

- Do you have any strong memories linked to a particular smell?

- How do you want people to remember you?

- What do you wish you were better at remembering?

- Are computers making our ability to remember better, or worse? Give some examples.

- How much do you think memories change over time?

- Why do you think some people remember the same events differently?

- Is the ability to memorize lots of things important? Why or why not?

Money

- Are you good at saving money?

- Do you think it's possible to have too much money?

- How much money per month does someone need to live comfortably?

- What do you think about the design of your country's money?

- The world is slowly shifting from a cash based money system to an electronic based money system. Is this a good or bad thing?

- Do you prefer to use cash or cards?

- Paying with phones is also becoming more popular. Is this better than cash or cards?

- Do you trust banks?

- Do you agree or disagree with the proverb "Money is the root of all evil"?

- What are some of the advantages and disadvantages of a barter system versus money?

Motivation

- What motivates you? Why?

- Are you very motivated to do things or do you need motivation?

- What activity do you have no motivation to do?

- What is a great motivational quote?

- Have you read any good motivational books or articles? What were they about?

- Does motivation come from inside a person or from their environment? Explain why you think so.

- How can you help someone who has no motivation?

- How often do you exercise or workout? What is the best way to motivate yourself to work out?

- What song do you listen to for motivation?

- What do you think of motivation posters in offices? Do they actually help?

Movies

- What is your favorite genre of movie?

- Who are some of your favorite actors?

- What kind of movie is best for a date?

- Do you cry during movies?

- What is the best movie you have ever seen?

- What is the scariest movie you have ever seen?

- How often do you watch movies?

- Do usually watch movies at the theater or watch them at home?

- Do you buy DVDs or download movies?

- What is the best snack to eat during a movie?

- What is the rudest thing someone can do during a movie?

- Which is more important, acting or special effects?

- If you could make a movie, what would it be about?

- If someone made a movie about your life, what kind of movie would it be?

Multiple Intelligences

- Howard Gardner created the theory of multiple intelligences. The theory says that there are 8 different types of intelligence:

  Logical-mathematical, spatial, linguistic, bodily-kinesthetic, musical, interpersonal, intrapersonal, and naturalistic

- Can you name two jobs that would be ideal for each intelligence category?

- Which one do you think you would score highest for?

- If you could choose one for your child to have, which one would you choose?

- Which do you think is the most likely to improve the world?

- Which intelligence is the one that is usually thought of as the most important?

- Which one is the least important?

- Which intelligence is the hardest to measure? How about the easiest one to measure?

- If you had people who each had high intelligence in one area, which would make the most money?

- Do you think that people can be labeled a "genius" if they score very high for one of these intelligences?

- Do you agree with Gardner's theory of multiple intelligences? Why or why not?

Music

- Who are your favorite bands or artists?

- How often do you listen to music?

- When was the last time you bought a song or album?

- Have you ever illegally downloaded music? Do you think it is okay or not okay to download music illegally?

- What kind of music do you listen to when you want to dance?

- What kind of music do you listen to when you are sad?

- Is there a certain song or type of music that makes you really energetic?

- Do you think music is getting better or worse?

- What kind of music will/do your kids listen to?

- What music did your parents listen to?

- How do you feel about your country's traditional music?

Natural Disasters

- How many types of natural disasters can you name? Which is the worst?

- What natural disasters are common in your country?

- Have you ever been through a natural disaster? Tell your group about your experience if it isn't too traumatic.

- Think of three natural disasters. What can you do to stay safe during and after those natural disasters?

- Do you know the difference between a hurricane, a typhoon, and a cyclone?

- Which country has the most natural disasters?

- Would you ever volunteer to help after a natural disaster hit? If yes, what would you like to volunteer to do? If not, why not?

- How can technology lessen the damage caused by natural disasters?

- Can natural disasters ever be a good thing?

- What do you think about people who follow tornadoes around to get data, video, and photographs?

- Can you think of any country that doesn't have natural disasters?

Natural Wonders

- What are the three most famous natural wonders in your country?

- What natural wonders are in danger from climate change?

- Should humans try to protect natural wonders? If humans protect natural wonders, are the wonders still natural?

- Have you ever been to a natural wonder?

- What makes something a natural "wonder"?

- What are three natural wonders you would like to see before you die?

- Should people be allowed to visit a natural wonder if the visitors hurt the natural wonder just by visiting it?

- Do natural phenomena (i.e., the aurora borealis) count as natural wonders? How about things like thunderstorms?

- Are natural disasters like volcanoes and earthquakes also natural wonders?

- How many countries with natural wonders can you name? Which country do you think has the most natural wonders?

- Would you rather visit natural wonders or manmade wonders?

Neighborhoods

- Did you like your neighborhood where you grew up?

- Where is the best place to eat in your city?

- Where is there a lot of crime in your city?

- What is the worst thing a neighborhood can have?

- Where is the best place to shop in your city?

- What did you think about your neighbors when you were growing up? Did you have any weird or odd neighbors?

- What did you like most about the neighborhood you grew up in?

- What kind of neighborhood do you want to raise your children in?

- Do you think it should be the government's responsibility to clean up neighborhoods or are the people in the neighborhood responsible for cleaning it up?

- What will neighborhoods be like in the future?

Neighbors

- What do you think of your neighbors?

- Is there anything that your neighbors do that annoys you?

- Did you play with kids who were your neighbors when you were a kid? Do you still keep in contact with them?

- Here is an idiom: "Good fences make good neighbors" What do you think it means? Do you agree?

- Do you think that neighbors were friendlier to each other in the past or are they friendlier now? Is this a good or bad thing?

- Have you ever asked to borrow something from your neighbor? Has your neighbor ever borrowed anything?

- What kind of person would be the perfect neighbor? Name at least three characteristics.

- How are countries that border each other similar to neighbors?

- Do you trust your neighbors? Would you leave them a key to your house?

- Think back in your life. Who was your most memorable neighbor?

News

- Where do you get your news from?

- How important is it for people to follow the news?

- Do you think that news agencies sometimes tell lies to make a story more popular?

- How much do you trust newspapers, television news, and news from the internet? Which is the most reliable source of information?

- What kind of news stories interest you the most?

- Do you think the news is too depressing?

- How has technology changed the way we consume news? How has it changed how the news is reported?

- What is the purpose of news companies in society?

- What do you think about how the news is reported in your country?

- Should news be more entertaining or informative?

- Would you ever consider getting a job in the news industry?

Numbers

- Who invented the number system we use today?

- What do you know about the history of numbers?

- Why are numbers so important?

- What are the two most important numbers in the world?

- Some people say that math is the language of the universe. Do you agree? Why or why not?

- What is your favorite number? Why is it your favorite number?

- What numbers are unlucky?

- Should students be allowed to use calculators to do math in school or should they learn to do it without calculators first?

- Do you know anything about the Fibonacci sequence?

- What is the first thing you think of when you think of three?

Online Dating

- Can two people fall in love over the internet without meeting each other first?

- How acceptable is online dating in your country?

- What are some of the good and bad things about online dating?

- Do people lie or mislead people on social networks?

- Do you know anyone who has tried online dating? How did it go?

- Do you think online dating will get more or less popular?

- Do you think that dating is better than arranged marriages?

- How have smart phones changed online dating?

- What are some popular online dating sites in your country?

- What do you think about people who date on MMORPGs (Massively Multiplayer Online Roleplaying Games)?

The Past

- What was your best memory from when you were a child?

- What is your earliest memory?

- What was your country like when you were a child?

- Do you think the past was better than the present? Why or why not?

- What were some of the benefits of living in the past?

- Where did you live when you were a child?

- Who used to be your hero when you were young?

- Did you have a pet? What was its name?

- Who were some of your favorite sports stars in the past? What did they play? Why were they your favorite?

- Name some of your country's famous sports stars of the past. Why were they famous?

- Talk about your country's past (100 years ago). How was the past different from the present? Food, weddings, clothing, school, work, recreation, communication?

Past Ability

- What was something that you were really good at when you were a kid but aren't good at now?

- What is something that you couldn't do at all when you were a kid but you can do really well now?

- When you were younger could you play soccer, cards, baseball, a musical instrument, or basketball? How good were you?

- "The older I get, the better I was." What does this idiom mean? Do you agree with it?

- What was something you wished you could do when you were a child?

- What are some childhood games you haven't played in many years?

- What is something you wish you had learned when you were younger?

- Ask your partner or group about what they could or couldn't do in the past.

- What is something that your parents did when they were children but your children won't be able to do?

- What is something you can do now but probably won't be able to do once you get older?

Personality

- Describe your personality.

- What kinds of people do you get along well with?

- What kinds of personality traits do you hate?

- How important is personality when you are choosing a spouse?

- Do all of your friends have similar personalities?

- What kinds of personality traits are best for running a business?

- What kind of personality should a doctor have?

- Is your personality more similar to your mother's or father's?

- Do you think we are born with our personalities or do we develop them because of what happens to us?

- What personality trait would you like to develop?

- Which of your personality traits would you like to lose?

Pets

- Do you have any pets now?

- Did you have pets when you were growing up? What were they? Do you remember their names?

- Are you a cat person, dog person, or do you like them both?

- Are pets good to have around children? What is the best pet for children to have?

- What are some strange pets you have heard of people having?

- Do you prefer small pets or large pets?

- How can having a pet help people?

- Why do some people want pets and others don't?

- Do you think that stray animals are a problem? If yes, what can be done to fix the problem?

- How did pets help people in the past?

- What exotic animal would you like to have as a pet?

Photography

- Do you use a camera or your phone to take pictures?

- How often do you take pictures of yourself?

- When you take a picture, do you usually take pictures with people in them or without people in them?

- Describe one of your favorite photos you have taken. What is in the photo? Why do you like it?

- Do you think people need to have expensive cameras to take good pictures?

- If you took photos as your job, what would you want to photograph?

- Do you think that digital cameras will totally kill film cameras? Why or why not?

- Do you know of anywhere near here that is good for taking pictures?

- Would you like to try underwater photography?

- What do you do with photos of old boyfriends or girlfriends?

- Why has photography become such a popular hobby?

Police

- Do you think police in your country have too much power or too little power?

- Is anyone in your family a police officer?

- What are the dangers of the police having too much power? How about the dangers of them having too little power?

- Do you think that most police are honest or corrupt?

- What kind of people become police officers?

- Have you ever been helped by a police officer?

- If you had enough police officers could you wipe out crime completely?

- Who are more important to the public, regular police officers or detectives?

- Have police been around since humans started living in cities? How have they changed over time?

- Do police make you nervous or do they make you feel safe?

Privacy

- How much do you value your privacy?

- Do you think that websites like Facebook take away too much of your privacy?

- Do you think people have the right to privacy? How about convicted criminals?

- The only people who need privacy are people doing something illegal. Do you agree or disagree? Why?

- Do you think the internet increases privacy or takes away privacy?

- What is the greatest threat to privacy?

- How private should corporations be? Should the public have access to corporate records?

- How transparent should a government be?

- Where do you like to go when you want to be alone?

- Should there be more or less security cameras around cities?

- How is privacy viewed in your culture?

Productivity

- Are you a very motivated person or do you wait until the last minute to do things?

- What technology helps you to be productive?

- Do you think that some people are more productive because of genetics or how they were raised?

- How can people improve their productivity?

- Who is the most productive person you know personally? How about really productive famous people?

- Do you think people today work harder than their parents?

- What are some things you want to do but don't have time for?

- What is the biggest waste of time for you?

- What advice will you/do you give your children?

- Do you think smart phones increase or decrease productivity?

- What do you think was the most productive period of your life so far?

Remedies

- What do you do when you have a cold?

- What ailments is western medicine better at curing?

- What ailments is eastern medicine better at curing?

- What do you do when you have a hangover?

- What are some old remedies you know of to help with ailments?

- What should you do to stop the bleeding if someone is hurt badly?

- What are some strange remedies you know of?

- Have you tried a strange remedy or cure before?

- Do hospitals make you nervous?

- What do you think the idiom "An ounce of prevention is worth a pound of cure" means? Do you agree with it?

- What is the best cure for a bad day?

Responsibility

- How involved should governments be in individuals' lives?

- Are criminals ever NOT responsible for the crimes they commit?

- What responsibilities do university students have? How about children or adults?

- At what age do you think someone becomes responsible for his or her actions?

- What should companies do to protect the environment?

- How much responsibility should individuals have for protecting the environment?

- Who has more responsibility for the environment, companies or individuals?

- What are some of your responsibilities?

- Who is responsible for taking care of the poor?

- Do you enjoy having responsibilities? Why or why not?

Restaurants

- What is your favorite restaurant near where you live?

- What is the best restaurant you have ever eaten at?

- What types of foreign food restaurants have you eaten at?

- Have you ever eaten at a restaurant abroad? What was it like?

- What (besides good food) makes a restaurant great?

- Do you prefer to eat at your parents' house or a restaurant?

- What is the worst restaurant you have eaten at?

- What is the strangest restaurant you have heard of?

- How do you feel about theme restaurants?

- Do you prefer darker or brighter interiors for restaurants? Why?

Retirement

- When is the average retirement age in your country?

- When do you want to retire?

- What do you plan to do when you retire?

- What do retired people do once they retire?

- Should the government, family, or the person retiring be responsible for a retired person?

- In your country what happens to retired people who can't take care of themselves?

- Where would you like to live once you retire?

- How do people save money for retirement in your country?

- Is it important to stay busy once you retire? Why or why not?

- Are you looking forward to retirement or would you prefer to keep working?

Science

- How can science help society? Does it hurt society in any way?

- What is the most important field of science? (Physics, chemistry, engineering, etc.) Why?

- Did you have any really great science teachers when you were a child or when you were in university?

- Should governments help fund science?

- What was the most important scientific discovery in the last 50 years?

- Think about your daily life. How do scientific discoveries affect your daily life?

- Should funding be given more to theoretical science or practical science, or should they be funded equally?

- Name some of the scientists you know of and what they are famous for.

- What are some things that scientists in your country have invented or discovered?

- Which scientific discovery has improved people's lives the most?

Seasons

- What is your favorite season?

- What do you think of when you think of winter?

- What are some things your family did when you were a child in spring?

- What is the worst season in your country?

- Does it snow in your hometown in the winter? Did you make snowmen when you were younger?

- What is your favorite thing to do in summer?

- What festivals or celebrations does your country have during the changing of the seasons?

- Do you ever go hiking when the leaves change in fall?

- Where is the best place to be in summer? How about winter?

- Does your country have a special food for any of the seasons?

Secrets

- Do you like knowing and finding out secrets? Why?

- Are you good at keeping secrets? Why or why not?

- Should governments keep secrets from their people? Why or why not?

- What kinds of secrets do you think your government has?

- What is something that lots of people dislike but you secretly love?

- Should husbands and wives keep secrets from each other?

- Should parents keep secrets from their children? If yes, what kind of secrets?

- What is a well-known secret?

- Do you know any secrets about celebrities?

- What kinds of secrets are dangerous?

- Can you tell us any of your secrets?

Shopping

- Where is your favorite place to shop for clothes?

- What products do you prefer to shop online for?

- What products do you prefer to shop in stores for?

- How do you feel about sales people following you and helping you when you shop?

- What makes a pleasant shopping experience?

- How do you feel about shopping at department stores or malls?

- What is your favorite ecommerce site? Why?

- Do you know anyone who is addicted to shopping? Are you addicted to shopping?

- Have you ever bought any counterfeit products like fake designer bags, clothing, or jewelry?

- Do you enjoy shopping for other people?

Singing

- How good are you at singing?

- Where do you sing most (e.g., shower, car, while doing housework, etc.)?

- How often do you do karaoke?

- What song are you best at singing?

- What song do you have to sing along with when you hear it?

- Whose singing do you hate?

- Can you sing your country's national anthem?

- Who is the best singer you personally know? How about the worst?

- Can singing be learned or are people born with the ability to sing?

- When was the last time you sang in front of someone?

Single Life

- What are some of the differences between married life and single life? Are the differences the same for men and women?

- What are the pros and cons of single life?

- Are you single or in a relationship? Do you wish you had a different relationship status?

- Why do some people choose to remain single?

- Who are some famous people who are single?

- Are there more single people in the city or the countryside?

- Are most of your friends married or single?

- Do you ever try to set your single friends up on dates?

- How do your habits change when you are single versus when you are in a relationship?

- Do you have any friends who love being single or who can't stand being single?

Sleep

- How many hours of sleep should people get every night?

- How many hours of sleep do you get every night?

- What do you do when you can't fall asleep?

- Have you ever fallen asleep at an inappropriate time?

- What is the minimum amount of sleep you can get and still be okay?

- Why do people sleep? What does it do to your brain?

- Do you know of anyone who talks in their sleep?

- Does anyone in your family sleep walk?

- Is it better to take many naps or get your sleep all at once?

- Do you think people get more sleep now than in the past?

- What are some things that can keep you from getting enough sleep?

Smoking

- Does smoking make you look cool? Why or why not?

- How many friends do you have who smoke? Do you smoke?

- Should people be allowed to smoke in public? If so, where?

- Is raising the price on cigarettes a good way to get people to quit?

- What do you think about electric cigarettes?

- What are some bad things about smoking?

- Are there any benefits of smoking?

- Should smoking cigarettes be illegal?

- How popular is smoking in your country?

- Should smoking be banned in movies? Why or why not?

Sports

- What are some sports you like watching? Why?

- What are some sports you dislike watching? Why?

- Do you play any sports? If so, which ones?

- Would you like to learn how to play a sport or do an activity? What would you like to learn?

- Why are sports so popular?

- Do you know of any interesting or strange sports or activities?

- What two sports would you like to mix?

- Do you prefer to watch sports or play them? Why?

- What do you think is the most dangerous sport?

- What do you think of athletes making so much money? Is it a good thing or a bad thing?

Stories

- What are the best kinds of stories? (i.e., funny stories, ghost stories, amazing stories)

- Who told you stories when you were a child? What kind of stories did they tell?

- What are some famous stories from your country? Do they teach the listener/reader something?

- There are many ways to experience a story. For example: Book, movie, TV show, spoken, radio, podcast, video game. What is your favorite way to experience a story?

- What is your favorite story?

- Tell your group a scary story.

- Tell your group a true story that happened to you.

- Tell your group a funny story.

- Tell your group a story that you heard when you were a child.

- Tell your group an unbelievable story.

- Tell your group a story with a moral lesson in it.

- Tell your group a story from history.

Stress

- How stressed are you? Why?

- How do you relieve stress?

- What are some other ways people relieve stress?

- Do you think people are more stressed now than in the past? Why or why not?

- What is the most stressful thing you can imagine?

- What could someone do to live a stress free life?

- When are you least stressed?

- How bad is stress for your health?

- Is stress sometimes good for people? Why or why not?

- How much stress should children have as they are growing up?

Success and Failure

- Describe a successful person.

- Is your idea of success the same as your parents' idea of success?

- Do you think people focus too much on appearing to be successful?

- Why is money the most common way of judging success?

- How much pressure do your parents put on you to be successful?

- How much pressure will you put on your children to be successful?

- Have there been any failures that made your life better?

- Is there a right time to give up and stop trying or should you never give up?

- Can you think of any famous people who failed spectacularly at something?

- Talk about a time you failed at something you tried. Don't talk about anything that will make you uncomfortable or embarrassed.

- Can you think of any famous quotes or idioms about success or failure?

Super Heroes

- Who is your favorite super hero? Why?

- What super power would you like to have?

- If you had super powers would you be a super hero or a super villain?

- Do you prefer dark super heroes like Batman or purely good super heroes like Superman? Why?

- Does a person's favorite super hero tell you anything about their personality? What does your favorite super hero say about your personality?

- Are there any real super heroes?

- What is your favorite super hero movie?

- Why have super hero movies become so popular?

- Do you think comic books are good or bad for children?

- How have super heroes changed over the years?

The Supernatural

- What supernatural things do you believe in (ghosts, ESP, fortune tellers, etc.)?

- Do you think science will ever prove any supernatural beliefs?

- What supernatural beliefs are unique to your culture?

- What are some of the scariest supernatural movies?

- What supernatural thing do you fear?

- Why do so many people believe in supernatural things that can't be proven?

- What are some supernatural holiday beliefs in your country?

- Where are supernatural occurrences most often reported?

- Do you think some people have supernatural abilities?

Technology

- Talk about how technology has changed in your lifetime.

- What do you think has been the most important new invention in the last 100 years?

- Are there any new gadgets that you really want to get?

- What do you think will be the next biggest technological advance?

- How can countries help to create more inventors?

- What is your favorite piece of technology that you own?

- How will computers change in the future?

- Do you think there will be more or less new innovation in the future? Why?

- Is there a piece of technology that you really want that doesn't exist? (Flying cars, teleportation, etc.)

- Give some examples of technology that have made the world worse.

- What do you think is the most important thing that humans have created?

- Do you think that people will travel outside of our solar system? How will they get there?

- Do you like new gadgets or do you prefer to use technology you are comfortable with?

- What are the possibilities of technology in clothing?

Television

- About how many hours of TV do you watch every day?

- What are some of your favorite shows?

- Do you like any foreign TV shows?

- What is the funniest show on television?

- Do you think people watch too much television?

- Are TV shows getting better or worse? Why do you think so?

- Would you like to be on TV? Why or why not?

- Do you have a favorite channel?

- Do you have cable or satellite television?

- Can you recommend a TV show to your classmates?

- What is the best drama on TV now?

Tipping

- Is it customary to tip in your country? If so, when should people tip? If not, should people start tipping?

- Does tipping actually improve the service you get?

- What is a reasonable amount to tip a waiter? How about a taxi driver?

- In which countries is it customary to tip? How about countries where it isn't customary?

- Do you like tipping or dislike tipping? Why?

- Talk about a time you felt like you had to tip someone when you didn't want to.

- Who deserves a tip but doesn't get one?

- How do you think tipping started?

- When you travel to a country, do you follow the local customs or your country's customs when you decide whether to tip or not?

- Who do you wish you didn't have to tip? Why?

Tourism

- How important is tourism in your country?

- What is the biggest tourist destination in your country?

- What are the benefits of international tourism? Are there any drawbacks?

- Do you prefer tourism package tours or do you prefer to plan your own vacations? Why?

- Is it better to go to popular tourist destinations or lesser known tourist destinations? Why?

- Should a government try to improve domestic tourism or try to attract international tourists instead? Why?

- What's the best way to travel when you visit a country? Train, car, bicycle, bus, some other way? Why?

- If you could create a tourism slogan for your country, what would it be?

- What's the best way for a country to bring in more tourists?

- How do you feel about tourists who visit your country?

Transitions

- What are the biggest transitions in an average person's life?

- What stage of life were you most happy to move away from?

- Which was better for you, elementary school, junior high school, or high school? Why?

- Did you study hard in high school?

- How would you change your life if you could?

- Starting university was a big transition. What are some of the good things about starting university? What are some of the bad things?

- One of the biggest transitions for people is marriage. What are some of the good and bad things about marriage?

- How will your life change after you have children? If you have children, how has your life changed?

- What do you think are the biggest transitions in a person's life? Which is the most important?

- What kinds of problems did you have when you went from elementary school to junior high?

- When does a child become an adult?

Travel

- Where are the best places to go for adventure vacations, history based vacations, shopping vacations, party vacations, or relaxing vacations?

- Where do you like to go on vacation?

- Where would you like to go on vacation?

- What are some things you must or have to do when you go on vacation to another country?

- What are some things that you must not or can't do on an airplane or in an airport?

- Tell your partner about your best travel story.

- What are some things you always take with you on a trip?

- Do you prefer package tours or making your own trip?

- Where did you spend your last vacation? What did you do?

- What are some of the benefits of travelling alone?

- What are some of the benefits of travelling with a group?

- What is the longest journey you have ever made?

University

- Did you or do you enjoy going to university?

- Some people say that the connections you make in university are more important than the education you receive. Do you agree or disagree?

- Many universities are putting classes online for free. How will this change education?

- Should a university education be free?

- What do you think about the university system in your country?

- Do you think a master's degree is worth the time and money? How about a PhD?

- What is the top university in your country? Why is it considered the best?

- What are the best degrees for job security?

- Do people need degrees to be successful? Can you think of people who are successful who don't have a degree?

- Many people are getting fake degrees or degrees from fake online universities. Will this have an effect on the job market and education? If so, what will the effect be?

Water

- How much water do you drink every day?

- How many glasses of water should people drink every day?

- How long can a person live without drinking any water? How long have you gone without drinking anything?

- Can you swim? How often do you go swimming?

- Where is a good place to go swimming near here?

- Try to name ten water sports.

- Not being able to get clean drinking water is a big problem in many places. What are some ways we can help people get clean drinking water?

- Think of the biggest river in your country. How polluted is it? Would you swim in it?

- Where does the biggest city in your country get its clean water from?

- The world's population is increasing rapidly. Getting clean water for everyone might become difficult in the future. Think of three ways we can avoid this problem.

Weddings

- How many weddings have you been to?

- Have you ever taken part in a wedding?

- What is the best part of a wedding?

- What are weddings like in your country?

- Why do you think weddings are universal among almost all cultures?

- "Going to a wedding is the making of another." What does that proverb mean? Do you agree?

- How do people celebrate after a wedding?

- What colors are most often used in weddings in your country?

- What do you think of arranged marriages?

- What is the worst thing about weddings?

- What food is traditionally served at weddings in your country?

Wishes

- If you could have three wishes that would come true, what would they be? (No, you can't wish for more wishes.)

- What do you wish you could change about the world?

- Many cultures throw things into water (like coins into a fountain) and make a wish. Why do you think people do that?

- What do you wish you could do after this class?

- What do you wish you could eat right now?

- What do you wish would happen today?

- When do people make wishes in your culture? (Shooting star, birthday, etc.)

- Have any of your wishes ever come true?

- Do you ever wish you could travel back in time?

- What do you wish you had right now?

ENJOY THE BOOK?

Check out our other books

We are always working on more books. You can find the PDFs for our other books on our website (eslconversationquestions.com) or paperback and Kindle versions on Amazon.

You can also ask your local book store if they carry our books.

ESL Role Plays: 50 Engaging Role Plays for ESL and EFL Classes

500 Grammar Based Conversation Questions

ESL Worksheets and Activities for Kids

IELTS Study Guide: Tips, Tricks, and Strategies

Or why not leave a review?

Every review makes a big difference. Reviews help other teachers find our books. So if you think this book can help others, let them know by leaving a review. I really appreciate it!

Plus, if you leave a review, you can join our review club and get free review copies of our new books and other books in our growing collection. You can find out more in the extras section at the beginning of the book.

We love feedback!

Do you have a recommendation for what book we should work on next? We would love to hear it. Have an idea for how we can make our books better? Let us know!

You can email me at: **larrypitts@eslconversationquestions.com**

Made in the USA
Las Vegas, NV
05 November 2024

11201335R00083